Nurses at Work

by **Karen Latchana Kenney**
illustrated by **Brian Caleb Dumm**

Content Consultant:
Judith Stepan-Norris, PhD
Professor of Sociology, University of California, Irvine

DISCARDED

magic wagon

Meet Your Community Workers!

visit us at www.abdopublishing.com

Published by Magic Wagon, a division of the ABDO Group, 8000 West 78th Street, Edina, Minnesota 55439. Copyright © 2010 by Abdo Consulting Group, Inc. International copyrights reserved in all countries. All rights reserved. No part of this book may be reproduced in any form without written permission from the publisher.

Looking Glass Library™ is a trademark and logo of Magic Wagon.

Printed in the United States.

Manufactured with paper containing at least 10% post-consumer waste

Text by Karen Latchana Kenney
Illustrations by Brian Caleb Dumm
Edited by Patricia Stockland
Interior layout and design by Emily Love
Cover design by Emily Love

Library of Congress Cataloging-in-Publication Data

Kenney, Karen Latchana.
  Nurses at work / by Karen L. Kenney ; illustrated by Brian Caleb Dumm ; content consultant, Judith Stepan-Norris.
      p. cm. — (Meet your community workers)
  Includes index.
  ISBN 978-1-60270-651-4
  1. Nurses—Vocational guidance—Juvenile literature. I. Dumm, Brian Caleb, ill. II. Title.
  RT82.K44 2010
  610.7306'9—dc22
                              2009002393

Table of Contents

Being a Nurse

Are you sick or hurt? A nurse is someone who will help you get better. To do this, a nurse asks questions about how you feel. Nurses give tests to check your body. They take your temperature and check your blood pressure.

Nurses help care for patients in hospitals. They watch for problems and give medicine to patients. Nurses bandage cuts. Nurses also write a patient's care in a health record.

Helping Others

Nurses help many people. Certain nurses help different groups. A neonatal nurse takes care of babies. Registered nurses, or RNs, help patients in the emergency room and the hospital. Other RNs help doctors during surgery. Licensed practical nurses, or LPNs, often help patients in long-term care facilities.

Nurse practitioners can write orders for some medicines and give care similar to a doctor's.

Nurses teach patients what to do after leaving the doctor's office or hospital. Patients need to know what to eat and how to take care of cuts. Nurses tell them what medicine to take and how often to take it. These important facts help patients get well.

At Work

You can find nurses in many places. They work in hospitals and doctor's offices. They work in long-term care facilities and nursing homes. Nurses can be found in schools and at summer camps. Sometimes a nurse works in a patient's home. Prisons and military bases also need nurses.

EMERGENCY

13

Nurses work with many people. They work with doctors or other medical workers. At work, most nurses wear nursing scrubs. These are loose clothes that are easy to keep clean.

Problems on the Job

Some patients have diseases. Nurses have to be careful not to get sick. Nurses work long hours. Sometimes they work overnight or on holidays. They stand for many hours. It can be tiring to work as a nurse.

Sometimes a nurse must be "on call." This means they have to be ready to work on short notice.

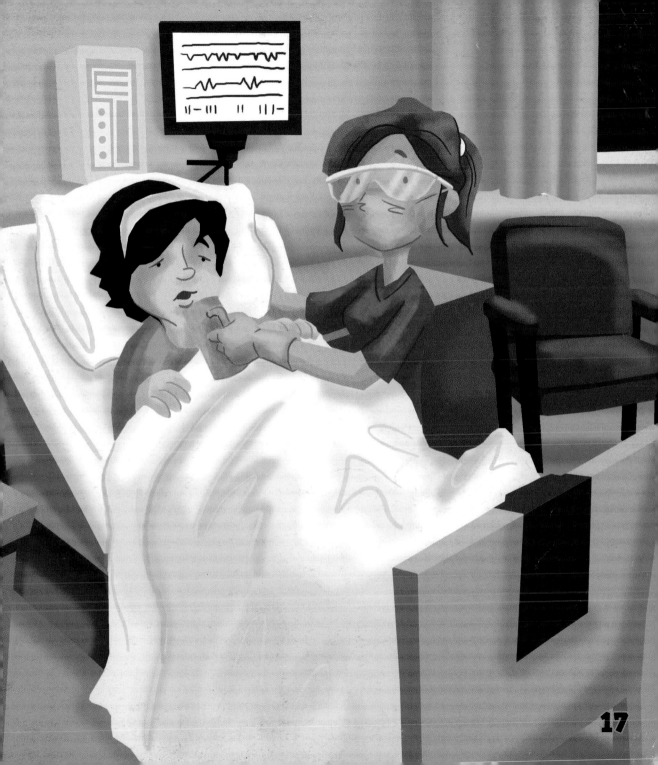

17

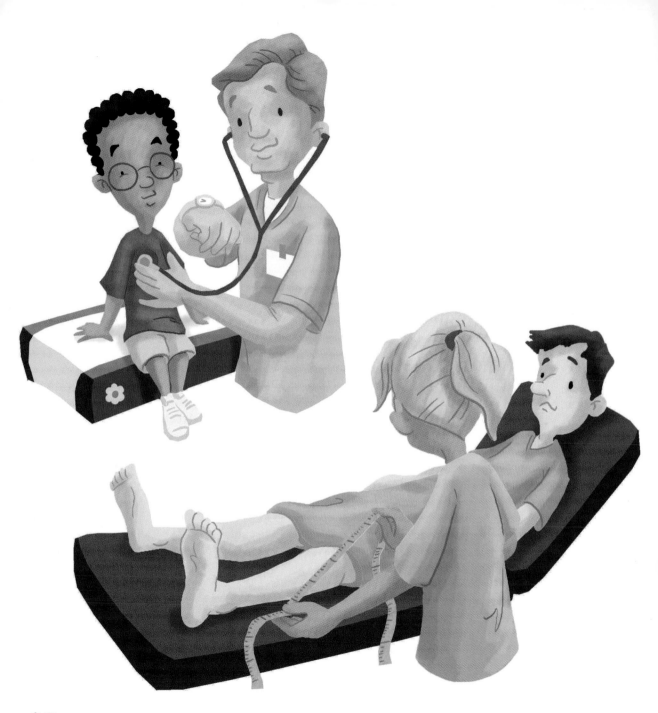

Tools Nurses Need

A stethoscope helps a nurse listen to a patient's heart and body sounds. To count a patient's heart rate, a nurse looks at a watch. A tape measure is used to measure parts of a patient's body.

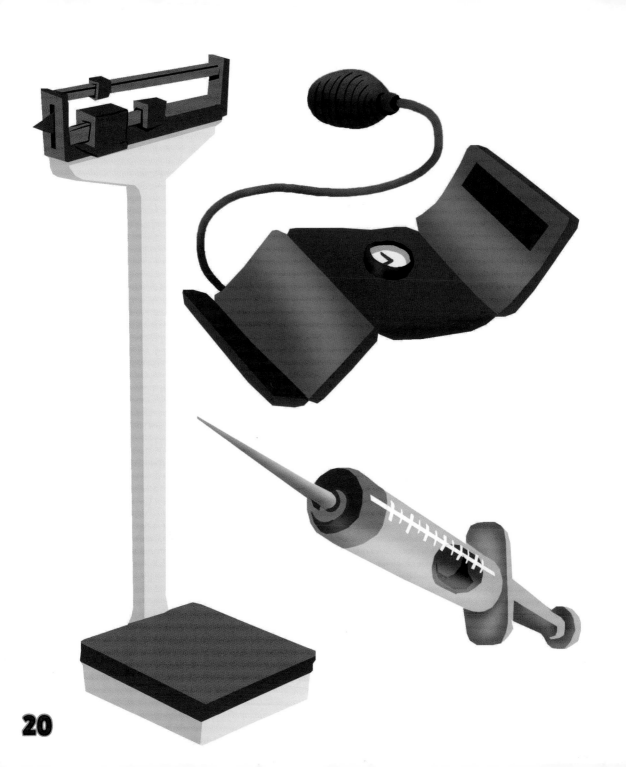

A nurse uses a scale to check a patient's weight. A thermometer measures a patient's temperature. A nurse uses a needle and syringe to give a shot. A blood pressure monitor is used to take a patient's blood pressure. These are just some of the tools a nurse uses every day.

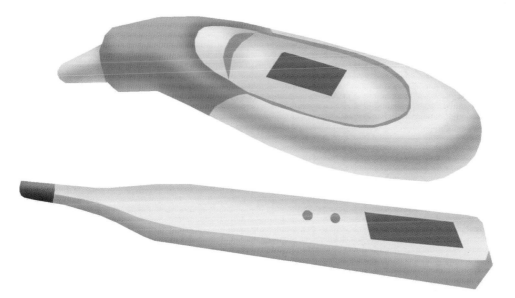

Technology at Work

Computers are important to nurses. They hold the health record of a patient. Nurses also use different machines. A heart-lung machine keeps a patient's blood healthy. Monitors record a patient's heartbeat.

23

Special Skills and Training

Nurses need to be caring and kind. They must know how to stay calm in an emergency. Nurses work with many different people. So, good team and speaking skills are also important. Math skills are needed to count medicine and measure a patient's body.

To become a nurse, a person has to go to college or a nursing school. A student must pass a nursing license test. A nurse trains by working with patients.

Every year, nurses take more nursing classes. These classes teach nurses new medical facts and nursing methods.

Many nurses belong to unions. Unions help workers get fair pay and hours.

In the Community

Has a nurse ever helped you? Nurses help many people. In schools and camps, nurses treat kids who are sick or hurt. In doctors' offices and hospitals, patients get better with the help of nurses. Nurses are important workers in every community.

A Day as a Nurse

Early Morning

Start work at 6:00 AM at the hospital.
Check the computer to see which patients need medicine.
Visit patients and check on them.
Give patients their medicine.

Late Morning

Look at patients' health records on the computer.
Add facts to their health records.
See how patients feel.

Afternoon

Take blood from patients for tests.
Check patients for problems.
Get results of tests.

Early Evening

Give patients their medicine.
Add facts to patients' health records.
Follow doctor's orders for patients.
End the workday at 6:00 PM at the hospital.

Glossary

blood pressure—the force of the blood as it moves in a person's body.

disease—a problem in the body that makes a person sick.

license—a government certificate that allows a person to do something.

long-term care facilities—places where patients with daily care needs live.

monitor—a machine that keeps track of parts of a person's body.

patient—a sick person who is helped by a nurse or a doctor.

surgery—when a doctor works inside a person's body to make them better.

syringe—a tube that connects to a needle and is used to give medicine to a person.

temperature—how hot or cold a person's body is.

Did You Know?

Florence Nightingale was a famous nurse from the 1800s. She started a nursing school in England. She wrote a book that changed the way nurses work in hospitals.

James Derham lived in New Orleans in the 1700s. He worked as a nurse. Later, he became the first African-American doctor in the United States.

On the Web

To learn more about nurses, visit ABDO Group online at **www.abdopublishing.com**. Web sites about nurses are featured on our Book Links page. These links are routinely monitored and updated to provide the most current information available.

Index

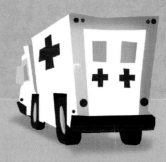